T0129635

THE PRACTICAL STRATEGIES SERIES
IN GIFTED EDUCATION

series editors
FRANCES A. KARNES & KRISTEN R. STEPHENS

Gifted Adolescents

Paula Olszewski-Kubilius, Ph.D.

Routledge
Taylor & Francis Group

NEW YORK AND LONDON

First published 2010 by Prufrock Press Inc.

Published 2021 by Routledge
605 Third Avenue, New York, NY 10017
2 Park Square, Milton Park, Abingdon, Oxon OX14 4RN

Routledge is an imprint of the Taylor & Francis Group, an informa business

Copyright © 2010 by Frances A. Karnes
and Kristen R. Stephens-Kozak

ISBN 13: 978-1-59363-401-8 (pbk)

Contents

Series Preface

The Practical Strategies Series in Gifted Education offers teachers, counselors, administrators, parents, and other interested parties up-to-date instructional techniques and information on a variety of issues pertinent to the field of gifted education. Each guide addresses a focused topic and is written by an individual with authority on the issue. Several guides have been published. Among the titles are:

- *Acceleration Strategies for Teaching Gifted Learners*
- *Curriculum Compacting: An Easy Start to Differentiating for High-Potential Students*
- *Enrichment Opportunities for Gifted Learners*
- *Independent Study for Gifted Learners*
- *Motivating Gifted Learners*
- *Questioning Strategies for Teaching the Gifted*
- *Social & Emotional Teaching Strategies*
- *Using Media & Technology with Gifted Students*

For a current listing of available guides within the series, please contact Prufrock Press at 800–998–2208 or visit http://www.prufrock.com.

Introduction

Adolescence is an interesting and important time for students, parents, and teachers. It is a long developmental period spanning from age 10 to 22 and encompassing the middle school, high school, and college years. It may be even longer for those gifted students who choose careers requiring further study and training beyond the bachelor's degree, often resulting in prolonged financial and emotional dependence on their families. Adolescence is a period of tremendous change and transition, both cognitively and physically, due to puberty and sexual maturation, as well as for social and psychological reasons.

The major task and challenge of the adolescent period is identity formation (Erikson, 1968). Adolescents must determine who they are by establishing their values, beliefs, talents, priorities, key attributes, and personality characteristics and how these influence and define their social roles, careers, and lifestyle choices. Adolescents move away from their families and the identities their parents and other family members may have prescribed for them toward those they have chosen for themselves based on who they want to be. Adolescents must find and establish an independent self. They must become autonomous, be responsible for themselves, and be able to take care of themselves. They must psychologically distance themselves from parents while still maintaining affiliation and connection. They must find meaningful work, establish their own intimate relationships, and begin to deal with the tensions that may exist between relationships and achievement. They take on new social roles during this period such as worker or girlfriend/boyfriend, and they must significantly redefine existing roles such as brother, sister, son, or daughter. An important question is whether the experiences of gifted adolescents during this time are significantly different than those of nongifted adolescents. Does being gifted alter the major developmental tasks of adolescence? Does it make this period of development easier or more challenging? How does the process of talent development unfold within this developmental period? What kinds of supports do talented adolescents need to ensure they stay on track and continue to develop their abilities during adolescence? What can educators and parents do to nurture their abilities? These questions and others will be addressed in this publication.

Talent Development During Adolescence

In order to understand the interplay between adolescence and giftedness, one must first understand what is important in terms of talent development during this period. During elementary school, a child's giftedness may become apparent to teachers and parents. Parents try to ascertain and nurture their child's interests and potential talents through out-of-school programs and activities. They watch, observe, and stimulate in the hopes of nurturing their child's talents. Teachers must be attuned to those students who require specialized programs to support their abilities and talents and refer such students for participation in gifted programs, if they are available.

It is in middle school, however, when talent development becomes even more focused. During these years, many schools move students into programs that are differentiated by content area, such as advanced math or language arts classes. This transition is consistent with the differentiation of gifted students' abilities that occurs as they grow older. As students progress through elementary school into middle school and high school, intellectual giftedness begins to receive less focus and relative areas of strength and weakness emerge. Adolescents generally have domains (e.g., verbal or math) in which they are stronger and perhaps more interested. This means that schools may group students into advanced math or language arts classes depending on their academic strengths. As they progress into high school, this kind of specialization continues, and students take honors and Advanced Placement (AP) classes in their areas of strength and interest.

As students move from the elementary years to middle and high school, specialization occurs both in terms of their abilities and the educational programs offered. Rena Subotnik (Subotnik & Jarvin, 2005) has proposed a stage model of talent development that offers a useful perspective for viewing how the talent development process changes as students age. According to this theory, there are several broad periods that comprise the talent development process. The first consists of the identification of ability, which through training and learning, develops into competence. During the second stage, further development of competence into expertise occurs, and in the third broad stage, the development of expertise into scholarly productivity or artistry in adulthood is initiated. The period of adolescence corresponds to stage 2 of this model and the beginning of stage 3. During this time, students are gaining knowledge and honing skills related to their talent area. They do this through courses in school, clubs, independent reading and work at home, and out-of-school programs. According to Subotnik, critical to this period is a student's (1) teachability or willingness to be taught and receive criticism, (2) motivation and desire to learn and achieve, (3) persistence in the face of challenges, (4) self-confidence, (5) ability to delay gratification, (6) ability to work and study independently, and (7) ability to set and work toward goals. In addition, students need to acquire tacit knowledge about educational paths and careers, so they can determine whether an occupation is a good match to their abilities and interests. Following this determination, students can make appropriate choices regarding courses, schools, and out-of-school activities. Mentors and contact with adult professionals working in the talent field are critical for providing tacit knowledge that can be acquired through authentic work experiences via apprenticeships, internships, or job shadowing.

Critical Issues for Gifted Adolescents

Identity

Although the main developmental task for all adolescents, regardless of ability, is the formation of a unique identity, this process has some special challenges for gifted adolescents. Research has shown (see Hébert & Kelly, 2006) that identity formation can occur more rapidly for gifted adolescents, and what may look like a premature decision in terms of a career or lifestyle may in fact be well thought-out and genuine. Identity formation also may be more complex for gifted adolescents who will have to determine who they are and what they want to do in light of high expectations for achievement and career choice held by their family and teachers. What if a gifted adolescent does not aspire to go into the family profession of law, medicine, or politics that generations before him or her have entered? Some families have strong histories of involvement in particular fields (e.g., the Kennedy family in politics and public service), and there can be a great deal of pressure for children to continue these traditions. What if the gifted adolescent aspires to a less prestigious career or occupation than those of his or her parents? In previous generations, children typically moved up the same socioeconomic ladder as their parents; however, this may no longer be possible in our current society. Adolescents may reject their parents' values of high paying, stable, conventional, and prestigious careers.

How will students who are so used to meeting the expectations of others with regard to their grades and accomplishments now set their own course and please themselves? Gifted adolescents who have defined themselves narrowly and primarily in terms of their achievements may need support and guidance to discover other important personal aspects central to their identity. They may fear the loss of affection and admiration of significant others if they eschew traditional achievement-oriented, high-status professions and careers. Pulling away from the family toward a more independent identity may be especially difficult for adolescents who have depended heavily on parents to support and manage their talent development activities and whose parents have sacrificed much to secure these opportunities for their child.

The process of identity formation begins with self-knowledge and acceptance of one's most distinguishing attributes and characteristics, but there are some gifted adolescents who have not come to own their exceptional abilities (Cross, 2004). They may be hiding their talents or downplaying their abilities for fear of rejection by others, particularly peers. This may be evident in the various healthy (e.g., using participation in extracurricular activities to build peer networks) and unhealthy (e.g., denying their giftedness by underachievement) ways students choose to cope with their giftedness (Swiatek, 1998). Some adolescents may be quite ambivalent about their giftedness, receiving both praise (from parents and teachers) and admonition (from peers) for their exceptional achievements. Gifted adolescents need support to come to terms with their giftedness, talents, and features of their personality in order to define an independent, autonomous self.

Peer Relationships

Having friends who are supportive is related to positive adjustment during adolescence and predictive of achievement and psychological health (Robinson, 2008). Friends are important and adolescents typically value their friendships very much. A major occurrence during adolescence is a broadening of a student's social networks and social contexts. This often means that others besides family members take on increasing importance in his or her life. Typically, the opinions of peers matter as much as those of family members. The problem for gifted adolescents has to do with their definition of a peer. For them, peers are not exclusively chronological age-mates but often include older students and adults who share similar interests and levels of expertise in an area. Their basis for friendship is the same as for adults—commonalities and shared interests; however, finding this among chronological peers may be difficult given gifted adolescents' advanced knowledge about topics and their passionate levels of involvement in their talent areas. As a result, one cannot assume that friendships will come from school or the neighborhood, particularly for gifted children who live in rural areas or attend small or low-performing schools. Other contexts outside of school may be the primary source for connecting with peers for many gifted adolescents.

Another issue for gifted adolescents regarding peers is the tension they often experience between acceptance by peers and academic excellence. The very things that earn them praise and reward from parents and teachers—high achievement, good grades, and high test scores—can earn them disfavor with their peers (Rimm, 2002). Gifted adolescents may come to believe that achieving and having friends are incompatible, depending upon the culture of their school, and that they must make a choice between the two. Adolescents find different ways to cope with this dilemma. For example, smart boys who are athletic and smart girls who are attractive may have an easier time gaining peer acceptance than more studious adolescents. Gifted girls often will participate in extracurricular activities as a way of gaining acceptance from peers, while others turn to the Internet to find friends or to out-of-school activities (Swiatek, 1998). Less effective coping strategies include denying one's gifted-ness or adopting a persona (i.e., class clown) to gain acceptance (Swiatek, 1998).

There is some evidence that gifted children desire deeper, more psychologically intimate relationships with just a few individuals rather than a wide circle of friends, which may be viewed negatively by other children (Coleman & Cross, 1988; Robinson, 2008). Because of this they may be perceived as loners or unfriendly or even arrogant or stuck-up. To maintain both peer acceptance and achievement, gifted adolescents may spend a great deal of time managing information about themselves to other children including keeping test grades and achievement information secret or feigning interest in topics to gain accep-tance from a group (Cross & Coleman, 2005). This can leave some adolescents feeling drained and wondering if they can ever just be themselves.

Finally, for some gifted students, the amount of time involved in practice and studying will necessarily decrease available time for socializing. Even the most dedicated adolescents may at times veer from or question their commitment to their talent develop-ment area in light of the commitment required. Some teens may need time off from a rigorous schedule to spend more time with friends. Ideally, talented teens can be involved in talent develop-ment activities that simultaneously provide for sustained peer interaction, but this may be difficult in talent areas that require more solitary study and those that involve competition with peers (e.g., tennis, ice skating).

Personal Characteristics

Introversion and extraversion are the opposite poles of a continuum and represent a basic and central dimension of human personality. Many people believe that intellectually gifted individuals tend to be introverted, although the research evidence about that is equivocal, with older studies finding a predominance of introverts in gifted samples and more recent work showing a fairly even split between introversion and extroversion amongst gifted students (Cross, Speirs Neumeister, & Cassady, 2007). Extraverts are typically enthusiastic, gregarious, seek out excitement and people, and typically are focused on what is going on around them. Generally, introverts are more reserved and less outgoing and social; prefer solitary and reflective activities; and are predominately interested in their own mental life. Introversion is more consistent with talent development, which typically requires the ability to spend time alone practicing, studying, reading, or honing skills and reflecting and analyzing one's own thinking. However, extraversion is more socially desirable in Western societies and may be particularly esteemed during adolescence (e.g., the popular social butterfly). Gifted adolescents who are introverted may feel they are out-of-sync with other adolescents, because they do not enjoy those social activities and events that are typical of adolescence and these differences can be a source of stress (Cross & Coleman, 2005). Where an individual stands on the extraversion–introversion continuum has implications for career or occupation choice, and problems may occur for those gifted students who are counseled into professions that may match their cognitive abilities and talent areas but do not mesh with important dimensions of their personalities.

Maureen Neihart (1999), a clinical psychologist who has worked extensively with and written about gifted adolescents, believes that sensitivity and intensity may be defining personality characteristics of gifted individuals. Sensitivity and intensity stem from an increased capacity of gifted persons to be stimulated by and responsive to external and internal stimuli, which have been called overexcitabilities. Overexcitabilities can be exhibited physically in rapid speech and compulsive talking; sensually via experiencing and seeking intense sensory experiences; intellectually through exceptional curiosity or truth seeking; through imagination with the frequent use of visual imagery and love of fantasy; and emotionally through intensified feelings and emotional reactions (see Daniels & Piechowski, 2009). Thus, the tendency toward overexcitability can be channeled and/or expressed in one or more different ways for gifted individuals but most typically in the emotional and imaginational domains.

Many gifted adolescents have strong emotional reactions to events or occurrences that other adolescents do not even notice (i.e., something tragic reported on the news). Gifted adolescents also exhibit advanced moral development and concern about ethical issues and fairness (Lee & Olszewski-Kubilius, 2006). These sensitivities and intensities combined with advanced moral reasoning may result in heightened states of anxiety, fear, or worry. They may not receive support for their reactions from peers or adults who tell them they are too sensitive and request that they "lighten up" or "chill out." They may feel exhausted by the emotional highs and lows traversed in a single day and may not know how to modulate and cope with these intense feelings and reactions. A desire for deep emotional intensity may lead some gifted adolescents to become involved in premature sexual relationships and early commitments. They may take on the emotional issues and needs of peers and family members at their own emotional expense (Daniels & Piechowski, 2009). Most importantly, emotionally sensitive gifted adolescents may feel they are different and not like others their age, and that such strong reactions are abnormal and bad. Gifted adolescents, especially boys, may resort to hiding their feelings in an attempt to fit in, which can result in increased emotional distress and somatic symptoms (Daniels & Piechowski, 2009). Gifted adolescents with imaginational overexcitability may wonder if there is something wrong with them or aberrant about their rich internal fantasy life and love of fantasy in books and movies. They may worry that their fascination with fantasy is juvenile and hide it from others. Helping gifted adolescents understand, appreciate, accept, cope with, and actually capitalize on these intensities (i.e., using their impressive imaginations to deal with abstract problems, generate creative solutions, or cope with difficult situations) is important for their overall psychological and emotional health and well-being.

Perfectionism is another personality characteristic of many gifted adolescents. There currently is a debate about whether there is any healthy form (e.g., striving for excellence) of perfectionism, but for the purpose of this publication, it is important to discuss the kind of perfectionism that involves the desire to be perfect, the fear of not being perfect, and the belief that one's acceptance as a person is dependent upon being perfect (Greenspon, 2006). Perfectionism is not a psychological disorder but, according to Greenspon, a personality constellation or a collection of behaviors, thoughts, and feelings. At the root of perfectionism is a self-esteem issue, as perfectionists believe that being perfect is the only way to gain acceptance and emotional connection to others. Certain environments are more likely to engender perfectionism in children, including (1) environments that are hypercritical and in which there is a great deal of anxiety about and demand for doing things the "right way"; (2) environments in which the message is that even though a grade or performance is good, it could always be better; (3) environments in which relationships are distant rather than warm and nurturing; and (4) environments that are dysfunctional and chaotic. Although gifted adolescents are not inherently more prone to perfectionism than their non-gifted peers, aspects of their early environments, such as high expectations from parents and the rewarding of perfect scores or grades by schools, are more likely to encourage the development of perfectionism (Greenspon, 2006). The roots of perfectionism almost always lie within the family, but the display of perfectionism typically is overtly seen within school, often in the form of underachievement as adolescents choose not to achieve at all rather than do so imperfectly. Perfectionism can be debilitating and derail a talented adolescent from the path of talent development. Reversing perfectionism requires counseling and therapy with the student and his or her family as well as the support of teachers and school counselors.

Another characteristic of gifted adolescents that has an effect on their decisions regarding courses to take, college majors, and career paths is multipotentiality. This refers to the often observed fact that many gifted individuals feel as though they have several different areas in which they are deeply interested and can achieve excellent levels of performance, but they may be overwhelmed by the thought of having to choose one area for a college major or career. There is some disagreement as to whether multipotentiality is as prevalent a problem as once believed, because research (Achter, Lubinski, & Benbow, 1996) has found that beginning in junior high, most adolescents show differentiation in their abilities with markedly more potential in one area over others. However, that does not negate the feeling that many adolescents have of being forced to give up an interest or activity they have spent years honing as they chose classes in high school or decide on a college, major, and occupation.

For example, consider Grace, who has been taking dance lessons since she was 3 years old, but who also is artistic. While taking dance classes at a local studio close to her home, one of her ballet teachers suggested to her mother that she seek out a better studio for Grace's lessons because of her natural ability in ballet. Grace also takes classes from practicing artists at a world-renowned art museum during high school, and her teachers encourage her to attend an art school for college. During the first few years of high school Grace continues to pursue both of these talents—dance and art—but because they involve a great deal of time outside of school for classes and lessons, she comes to the point where she feels she must choose one over the other. She is upset about having to make the choice and very fearful she will make the wrong one. In reality, Grace may not be equally talented in dance or art. She may have difficulty making the choice because she has not received judgments about her abilities from professionals with similar levels of expertise in each area (i.e., a teacher at a local dance studio versus a practicing artist at a selective art school), and thus she does not know her ability is much higher in one area than the other. If at all perfectionistic, she may be consumed with trying to determine the perfect choice at the age of 16. Also, like many gifted adolescents who have persisted with training in a talent area and demonstrate great motivation and perseverance, Grace will be very reluctant to sacrifice a dream or relegate a once-anticipated career choice to an avocation. Many gifted students who feel they have competing interests and abilities have not considered that other aspects of their personalities and values may be just as or more important than talent in making such choices. Some gifted adolescents will be frenetic in their efforts to keep all options open and become exhausted trying to maintain excellence in multiple areas. Helping gifted adolescents determine their real strengths and interests is key when addressing perceived or real multipotentiality.

Talent Development

A major challenge for some adolescents is maintaining commitment to their talent area through continued study and practice. This may be especially difficult during the adolescent period due to the importance placed on social activities and peer affiliation. Retrospective studies of eminent individuals have shown that for a variety of reasons, these individuals spent considerable time in their youth alone, working independently on activities related to their talent area (Olszewski-Kubilius, 2008). They were writing, drawing or painting, practicing music, or reading widely and voraciously. Such activities resulted in a great deal of skill development, and extensive, rich networks of knowledge that laid the groundwork for advanced levels of competence (Olszewski-Kubilius, 2008). Csikszentmihalyi, Rathunde, and Whalen (1997) studied adolescents who maintained their commitment to talent development (i.e., continued to take classes and participate in out-of-school and extracurricular activities) throughout their high school years and found that spending time alone to study or practice was a major challenge for many talented teens. They said:

> Talent development is easier for teens who have learned habits conducive to cultivating talent. For instance, talented students spent less time just socializing or hanging out with friends. Instead they shared more active and challenging pursuits with friends, for example, hobbies and studying. They learned to modulate attention: more concentration in school and less when socializing, doing chores, and watching TV. They also spent a greater amount of time alone, which is essential for anyone building future skills. More solitude and more productive activities probably accounted for more somber weekly moods than average teenagers. But talented teens had learned to tolerate negative moods and reported being more happy, cheerful, active and motivated than average teenagers when productively engaged. (p. 224)

The ability to spend time alone is dependent upon commitment but also on practice dealing with psychological isolation and developing mechanisms to stay connected while focused on work, study, and practice. Today's teens have many ways to achieve this including e-mail, instant messaging, and texting, but many struggle to balance social interaction with study and practice.

Big-Fish-Little-Pond Syndrome (BFLP)

Self-concept is another important aspect of personality. Self-concept typically is thought of as an individual's general perceptions, thoughts, and ideas about him- or herself as well as one's self-evaluations. It is, in reality, multidimensional, as most of us have different ideas about different aspects of ourselves—we are better in some areas than in others (Pyryt, 2008). Consequently, most assessments of self-concept have subscales such as social self-concept (how we see our interactions with others; friendships), physical self-concept (how we view our physical selves), and academic self-concept (how we view our performance on academic tasks; ability to learn). Only academic self-concept is strongly related to academic achievement and is both an outcome and precursor of high achievement (Marsh, Trautwein, Lüdtke, Baumert, & Köller, 2007; Pyryt, 2008). Gifted students who experience academic success are likely to evidence increases in their academic self-concepts. Positive academic self-concepts provide these students with the confidence to take on and per-severe through more challenging work.

There is considerable research to indicate that gifted students generally have higher academic self-concepts than nongifted students, probably as a result of many successful academic experiences and participation in gifted programs (Marsh et al., 2007). The reason for changes in academic self-concept is that a person's beliefs about how good he or she is in a particular area are determined, in large part, by comparisons to others at the same level. For example, a student who easily performs at the top of his or her class in junior high may have high academic self-concept. However, once he or she enters a different context, such as a large high school in which there are many other very talented students, a reevaluation based on individuals within the new social context will occur and the student's academic self-concept may decline. This phenomenon has been coined by Marsh and his colleagues as the Big-Fish-Little-Pond Syndrome and may result in the student being less confident and, therefore, less likely to pursue advanced courses, fearing that he or she cannot achieve top grades in rigorous classes in the new academic setting.

Jacqueline Eccles (2007) has proposed a model of what influences students' achievement-related choices (e.g., whether to take AP Calculus AB or AP Statistics) and suggests that self-concept is an important component of students' decisions. According to her model and research, an adolescent's academic self-concept affects his or her expectations for success and beliefs about the relative costs involved in selecting a particular course or college major. So, a student with lower academic self-concept may decide that his or her chance of getting a grade of A in AP Calculus AB is slim given that the class will be filled with many other mathematically talented students, and in desiring an A for his or her college applications, may decide to take a different, less rigorous course instead. Or, in Grace's case, she might feel that getting an A in AP Calculus AB is possible, but would require too much of her time given that she is planning on applying to art schools and needs to spend considerable time preparing a portfolio. Alternatively, if AP Calculus AB is regarded by the student as very important to his or her future because of plans to become a physicist or engineer, and he or she is confident that the hard work will pay off with a desirable grade, the student may go ahead and take the course. Academic self-concept is a result of many achievement-related experiences and previous history can be an important factor in making these decisions.

Declines in academic self-concept due to the Big-Fish-Little-Pond phenomenon are more likely to occur at transition points in schooling (e.g., from junior high to high school and from high school to college) and tend to affect students who have never experienced challenging academic classes. Some gifted students can easily earn high grades with little effort until they reach college, and only then do they find the work demanding. Without support and encouragement to persist through academic challenges and cope with the decline in academic self-concept associated with BFLP syndrome, some students choose to opt out of challenging courses of study or even drop out of school altogether.

How individuals cope with blows to their academic self-concept has a great deal to do with their views on learning and ability. Carol Dweck's research (2007) revealed that people who view abilities as a gift and fixed would question their ability and lose motivation when they encountered difficult courses or setbacks (i.e., a low test score or grade). In contrast, people who view their abilities as something that can be developed over time with hard work were more likely to seek out and find effective coping mechanisms and identify remedies and strategies to improve their performance when difficulties were encountered.

Unfortunately, many gifted students view their abilities as fixed and stable rather than malleable and developing. Even the word giftedness implies they have been given something they did not earn and often the messages received from well-meaning parents and teachers reinforce this notion: "You are so lucky you're so smart," or "Most students are not blessed with your abilities." Often, gifted students conclude that if they have to work hard to achieve, they must not be gifted. They equate giftedness with easy grades. When standards and expectations become higher, as they do in middle and high school, some gifted adolescents will flounder and adopt strategies to hide the fear and anxiety that result from threats to their self-concept and their perceived "loss of gifted ability."

Appropriate Benchmarking

As gifted students mature and progress through school, determination of talent will rest increasingly on achievement as opposed to ability or potential. For Cross and Coleman (2005), the label of giftedness cannot be applied to an adolescent unless there is evidence of achievement and involvement in the talent domain.

> Young children and preadolescent children who are gifted show high general cognitive ability, either through potential (ability), actions (performance) or rapid learning in school-related domains. By secondary school, gifted children should be demonstrating advanced development in a foundational domain or have produced works in some societally valued area and have demonstrated consistent engagement in activities associated with either type. (p. 59)

An issue for gifted adolescents, particularly those talented in performance areas such as art, music, and theater, is appropriate benchmarking of their talents and abilities or a realistic view of one's level of competency or development compared to other similarly talented adolescents. Many things contribute to students' difficulty in obtaining appropriate benchmarking including having little access to other talented students or teachers with high levels of talent or expertise. If a science teacher does not possess depth of knowledge in science, especially current science research methods and cutting-edge research topics, he or she will not be able to guide a student to produce a competitive project for the Intel Science Talent Search competition. If an art teacher does not have professional credentials in some area of art, he or she may not be able to facilitate an artistic student's development or steer him or her toward appropriate art schools. Lack of courses in school, extracurricular activities, and out-of-school programs may severely limit students' opportunities to gauge how they are progressing and what else they can do to further their talent development. Recall that Subotnik and Jarvin (2005) identified adolescence as the critical period when abilities identified in elementary school are developed into competencies and then into expertise. Competency must be easily seen and demonstrated for students to gain entrance into selective academic institutions and programs, art schools, and music conservatories that will enable them to progress toward scholarly productivity and creative artistry in adulthood. Increasingly, as talented students progress, they must have critical feedback from knowledgeable professionals in the talent domain.

Competition and Stress

Although gifted individuals often are admired and even envied for their exceptional abilities and achievements, the road to success is not always easy. Being a creative performer or thinker in a field requires a strong constitution. Research on eminent individuals shows that while many enjoy financial and other rewards from their achievements, they also must deal with high levels of stress and tension associated with shouldering a great deal of responsibility, risk-taking, and competition. Many highly creative and productive people seem to be able to tolerate and deal with unusual amounts of stress, in part, because they learned to cope with it at a young age (see Olszewski-Kubilius, 2008, for a discussion). One factor that promotes management of high levels of stress is a home environment where there is a balance between tension that results from high parental expectations for achievement and support through genuine caring and warmth among family members. Families push children to be independent, pursue their interests, and develop their abilities, yet keep them close psychologically and emotionally (Csikszentmihalyi et al., 1997). Another contributing factor is a school environment that gives students small doses of challenge and practice with increasingly demanding situations such as thorough, rigorous courses and competitions. As a result, students acquire a taste for challenge and may even seek it in their work (Olszewski-Kubilius, 2008). Learning techniques to deal with stress such as deep breathing, relaxation, and self-talk are critical coping mechanisms as are managing moods and maintaining a positive attitude (Neihart, 2008). Gifted adolescents must learn how to cope with the stresses and anxieties that come with high aspirations and achievement, as these are important ingredients to success.

Authentic Learning Experiences

Although it is true that gifted adolescents revel in abstract ideas and excel at critical and analytical thinking, not all are sufficiently motivated to remain committed to learning and talent development by the esoteric when it seems so far removed from real life. Some adolescents desire and need experiences in their talent field that mirror actual work and help demonstrate concretely how they would make a living in the area. Csikszentmihalyi et al. (1997) found that teens who were talented in science did not report enjoying their high school science and math classes, but nevertheless strove to do well in them because they believed these classes were useful to their long-term goals of becoming physicians or research scientists. Teens talented in the arts had just the opposite experience; they found their art and music classes intrinsically motivating on a day-to-day basis but did not perceive them to be useful toward their long-term goals. These authors suggested that talent development through the teenage years requires school experiences that are immediately enjoyable, fulfilling, and intrinsically motivating coupled with an understanding of how those classes address long-term, instrumental goals. For many teens and young adults, learning by doing, particularly learning from practicing professionals, is much more motivating and engenders both immediate enjoyment as well as long-term commitment. Witness the current popularity of vocational education for many teens and the history of apprenticeship training in many fields. Unfortunately, in the United States, vocational training often is reserved for students who are not succeeding in academics and/ or for students who do not plan on attending college—not academically gifted adolescents. All teens, including gifted teens, need glimpses of where they are going in order to determine the direction and nature of their path to get there. However, in our current educational system, adolescents are expected to keep working hard toward an often intangible, obscure goal. It should be no surprise when they give up along the way or are dissatisfied when they finally achieve it.

Gender Differences

Although the issues above affect all gifted adolescents, gifted girls and boys may face some unique challenges because of their gender, stemming primarily from societal expectations. For example, gifted girls generally receive better grades in school compared to gifted boys, but do not achieve as highly as boys in terms of their careers and occupations (Reis, 1998, 2006). Gifted women earn less than gifted men and have lower levels of attainment on almost any traditional (albeit male-defined) marker of success in our society (e.g., publications, patents, attendance at prestigious schools). Why is this the case?

A compilation of research (see Kerr, 1997; Reis, 1998, 2006, for a fuller discussion) suggests that young gifted girls are rewarded and positively reinforced for high grades and achievement. However, as they approach adolescence, the nature of the messages they receive from significant others often changes. In addition to or even in lieu of high achievement, girls are expected to groom themselves to be attractive and prepare to be wives and mothers. Kerr (1997) referred to this as the "culture of romance." As a result, gifted girls may experience a conflict between affiliation and achievement. They may try to fit in with their age-mates and be preoccupied with clothes, style, and dating—even when in their heart they are focused on school, achievement, and their own talent development. Gifted adolescent girls may have difficulty finding friends who share their interests and commitment to serious study or practice. They may experience real social isolation or feel psychological isolation as they feign interest in what they consider superficial activities as a means to cope with the typical high school peer culture. The emphasis on appearance during adolescence is difficult for all girls, but some gifted girls, rather than reject the culture of romance, may strive to have it all—good grades and high achievement, popularity, and physical attractiveness. Gifted girls prone to perfectionism may succumb to eating disorders in an effort to please everyone and maintain control over a life when there is too much pressure to achieve in all areas.

Gifted girls tend to be more self-reliant, assertive, and dominant than nongifted girls, and these typically are thought of as masculine characteristics (Olszewski-Kubilius & Kulieke, 1989). Thus, gifted girls may have difficulty reconciling their femininity with their desire to achieve, make a mark, or influence others.

In high school, gifted girls may get some relief from social pressures in a larger social context where they can find like-minded intellectual peers or inoculate themselves through participation in out-of-school programs. However, once girls enter college they may face new pressures. Karen Arnold (1995) conducted a landmark longitudinal study of high school valedictorians in the state of Illinois and found that as these gifted girls went through college, self-confidence in their abilities declined, as did their career aspirations. As the gifted young women pondered college majors in preparation for a career, they feared they would not be able to combine marriage and motherhood with a demanding occupation. Some gifted young women have not seen many role models in their immediate family as to how to effectively balance motherhood with high-level careers. Instead they see exhausted mothers who opt out of careers altogether or choose lower level jobs compatible with their families' needs and schedules. Even the most highly gifted girls expect to work part-time in the future, and gifted young men also expect their wives will have less prestigious careers and take primary responsibility for the family (Lubinski & Benbow, 2006).

Gifted boys face societal pressures, too, although of a different kind. Kerr and Cohn (2001) talk about the "boy code" that exists within our society emphasizing strength, silence, self-reliance, athleticism, daring, courage, violence, power, and dominance. Although gifted boys and girls tend to be more androgynous than stereotypically male or female, many gifted boys are deeply emotionally sensitive and intense, which does not fit with the boy code and may be viewed as feminine. Gifted boys whose personalities are at odds with the boy code may experience great difficulty reconciling their core personality characteristics with those that society expects from their gender (Kerr & Cohn, 2001). In addition, high schools may have little to offer gifted boys who are at risk of disengaging from school because current school culture is both highly anti-intellectual and feminized (i.e., athletic achievements are revered over academic ones and most leadership positions in extracurricular activities are occupied by girls).

Although society pressures girls to find husbands who are a "good catch," it simultaneously pressures gifted males to enter high status, prestigious fields and careers, even if these are not what they truly want to do or if they don't match their personalities and preferred lifestyles (Kerr, 1997; Kerr & Cohn, 2001). Gifted males might find it difficult to resist the temptations and rewards of such careers in lieu of less prestigious, lower paying, or less traditional jobs that are more fulfilling. In addition, gifted males are socialized to pursue the "perfect 10" (Kerr & Cohn, 2001) or trophy wife rather than a true companion and partner.

Another important gender difference for gifted males and females has to do with their attributions regarding their successes and failures. Gifted males tend to attribute their successes, whether in academics or athletics or other areas, to ability and attribute their failures to effort, while gifted females do the opposite (Dweck, 2006, 2007). Males' attributions are healthier because when they encounter setbacks and problems, the obvious solution is to increase or improve effort. When gifted females fail, the only conclusion to be drawn is that they are not as able as they thought. These differences in attributions stem from the different direct and indirect messages that gifted males and females have received from significant others, parents, and teachers throughout their lives (Dweck, 2006, 2007).

Culturally and Linguistically Diverse (CLD)

Although identity formation is a major developmental task for all adolescents, culturally and linguistically diverse students face some particular challenges in this area. These include developing a positive racial identity and self-concept, both necessary for high achievement, in the midst of potentially negative and debilitating experiences and messages.

Ford and Harris (1999) indicated that American schooling has largely centered on White, Western European ideas about what is appropriate curriculum. Our society in general tends to emphasize values (e.g., individualism as opposed to collectivism) and behaviors (e.g., moderate as opposed to intense emotional expression) consistent with these Western traditions. As a result, children from other backgrounds may feel that their cherished cultural values; ways of thinking and behaving; and their literature, art, music, and customs are inferior. Ford and Harris referred to this as "deficit thinking," which permeates our educational practices with respect to culturally and linguistically diverse students. Even the most well-intentioned teachers may give subtle messages to CLD students that their ways of doing things are not as good as the "right way," and they are not capable of high achievement. In addition, the lack of a truly multicultural curriculum can make it difficult for CLD students to experience a sense of belonging in school and receive validation as a scholar. Hence it is no surprise that many CLD students distance themselves from school early, are underrepresented in gifted programs, opt out of advanced programs and classes in middle and high school, and lose motivation to persist with high achievement as they progress through school.

CLD students must typically learn to exist within two worlds, that of their family and communities, and that of school and the larger society, each with different expectations regarding how people communicate and interact (Ford & Harris, 1999). CLD students must essentially learn to be bicultural, alternating their communication and behavioral styles depending upon the context. They must forge a positive racial identity in the face of implicit or explicit negative messages and cultural misunderstandings (Ford & Harris, 1999).

Scholars have identified several psychological and social factors that are operative for gifted CLD students but may not be present for non-CLD students. These include associating academic achievement with "acting White" and fearing that achievement will be perceived as rejection of one's culture and result in social isolation from peers and even family (Ogbu, 1992). In addition, they may fear that participation in high-stakes testing and achievement situations will confirm negative stereotypes about the achievement of one's cultural group (Steele, 1997). These beliefs may be the cause of underachievement and at the root of what Ford, Grantham, and Whiting (2008) and others (Mickelson, 1990) referred to as the attitude–achievement paradox, in which CLD students verbally endorse beliefs that education is vital to future success but put little effort into their schoolwork. CLD students may agree that in an ideal world, hard work and achievement in school will lead to occupational and financial success, but may believe it won't for them because of racism and inequities in society.

Gifted CLD students often find themselves one of only a handful of non-White or Asian students within a gifted program or AP or honors classes (Miller, 2004). They may feel they do not belong and that the teacher and other students have low expectations for them, or alternatively, they may feel pressure to perform exceptionally well because they are representing their entire racial or ethnic group. They may feel lonely and have to hide or defend their choice to make academics a high priority in their life.

Another challenge for many CLD students, particularly those who come from low-income families, is figuring out how to make their dreams a reality. Low-income CLD students aspire to careers they know about only from television or through books. They may be the first in their family to attend college and they may have had little opportunity for contact with adult professionals in their field of interest. As a result, they do not acquire the tacit knowledge about higher education (e.g., the best schools for their major) and career paths (e.g., what students can major in if they want to go to medical school) that more advantaged students receive from family members and others within their neighborhoods and communities (Arnold, 1995).

Suggestions for Educators and Schools

Challenging Coursework and Instruction

Gifted adolescents thrive on challenge. Only through challenge can students really grow. Challenge means that students engage in courses and instruction that is somewhat ahead of their current level of knowledge and skills—not so much beyond that they experience anxiety and feel overwhelmed, but ahead enough that they have to "reach" to succeed. Many middle schools offer special gifted programs and group students for accelerated courses in key content areas such as language arts and mathematics. High schools may offer honors and Advanced Placement courses. These options typically allow students earlier access to courses (algebra in middle school or an AP class in ninth grade) or more advanced versions of courses. These offerings will be sufficiently challenging for many gifted students, but not for all. Some gifted students' learning abilities require not only earlier access but also an accelerated presentation of coursework through fast-paced classes (e.g., compression of a year-long course into a shorter time frame) or grade telescoping (e.g., compression of several years or

grades of school into one). The most highly gifted adolescents
will need individualized programs of study that allow them to
move at their own accelerated pace through the curriculum.
Other options, such as early access to college though dual enroll-
ment or early entrance are needed for students who complete
the high school curriculum early.

Students who come from schools with few advanced offerings may need to supplement their in-school curricula with
courses obtained through distance learning programs, particularly ones designed specifically for gifted learners. Distance education programs also can be used to supplement and expand a
gifted student's high school coursework, particularly in a special
interest area (see Olszewski-Kubilius & Lee, 2008).

Challenging courses and programs of study not only enable
gifted adolescents to obtain knowledge and skills related to the
content area, but also promote study and organizational skills
and provide supportive environments in which students can take
intellectual risks. Such courses help students acquire coping skills
for handling challenging environments and stress. Classes with
other gifted students also promote appropriate benchmarking
of talent from which emanates increased commitment to talent
development and the setting of new goals. These programs and
courses also provide a context in which students can receive a
great deal of emotional and psychological support for being a
gifted student committed to study and achievement.

Authentic Work Experiences

Gifted adolescents begin to think about what career they
want to pursue in the future. For most, this is a very abstract
experience. In our society, we rarely involve adolescents in
"real work." At best, they are allowed to observe adults at work
through visits to parents' workplaces or through job shadowing
programs at school. They also may participate in mini-versions
of adult activities such as producing the high school newspaper.
These are helpful and desirable but not sufficient experiences for
many gifted adolescents.

There are many advantages to authentic work experience. Students get a realistic picture of what a career or job actually entails. How many females who are interested in science reject a career as a research scientist because of the mistaken notion that it is a lonely, isolating experience consisting of mostly laboratory work? In reality, most research scientists at major universities have graduate students do the lab work and they spend a considerable amount of their time writing grants and articles, managing large projects, supervising laboratories, and interacting and collaborating with other scientists. For gifted adolescents with many interests, authentic work experiences can help narrow their lists of possible careers to ones that are best suited to their personalities and abilities.

Another advantage of authentic work experiences for gifted students is the motivation and increased commitment they engender for study and practice in their area of interest. Many gifted adolescents can persist in book study as a means toward a desired end, but not all. Motivation can lag when the endpoint is unclear or only vaguely understood. Authentic work experiences give gifted adolescents contact with professionals who can provide advice and tacit knowledge about entering and preparing for a career. This is especially critical for adolescents who come from poor or working-class families and communities. Often, these same professionals become role models for students, helping them realize their dreams.

Early and Continued Career Exploration

Career exploration needs to start in middle school, as most gifted students are already thinking about possible careers at this point. Ideally, career exploration should proceed in stages beginning with learning about careers through books, Internet sources, professionals through talks at school or through interactions with the community, and from family members. During high school, students need deeper exposure through job shadowing arranged informally by students' families or through organized community or school programs. Preferably, students would have the option and opportunity to explore one or more careers in depth through an unpaid internship or mentorship while in the latter years of high school. Colleges and universities are increasingly involving students in internships early in their undergraduate studies. Career guidance and education needs to begin early, be continuous, and move from brief encounters to more sustained, in-depth experiences.

Sustained Access to Talented Peers

Gifted adolescents benefit from being able to spend significant amounts of time interacting with other gifted students with similar interests and levels of talent. Having friends is very important for all adolescents, as they can be significant sources of support and encouragement. For gifted adolescents, friends can buttress motivation and continued commitment to high achievement and inoculate students against a negative and anti-achievement peer culture. Opportunities to make friends require that students be together for extended periods of time, and gifted programs in middle school that pull students together for only several hours a week may not be sufficient to allow friendships to grow and develop. Homogeneous classes in middle school and honors and AP classes in high school can facilitate friendships among gifted students and extracurricular activities such as math clubs also can help. These experiences promote talent development by creating psychologically safe environments for gifted students, where they feel free to be themselves.

Students whose schools do not offer opportunities for sustained interactions with intellectual peers need to be steered toward community and other out-of-school programs such as university-based summer programs or summer or weekend programs offered through colleges, museums, and other organizations. Even distance learning programs can enable gifted students to have contact with other gifted students around the country.

Out-of-School Programs

Experts in gifted education agree that developing the talents of adolescents may not be entirely possible within the context of schools and traditional educational institutions (Olszewski-Kubilius & Lee, 2008; VanTassel-Baska, 2007). There are a variety of out-of-school programs that can supplement, complement, and enrich students' in-school courses and programs and specifically provide them with additional challenging courses to accelerate or broaden their school curriculum; increase their access to peers, adult role models, and mentors; and provide authentic work experiences and previews of careers and college. These include distance learning programs, summer programs, mentorships and internships, competitions, study abroad, and service learning programs. Each of these programs has benefits for gifted students (see Table 1) and may be especially important for students whose school offerings are limited or whose communities have few opportunities for talent development. School personnel and parents often are not aware of out-of-school programs and their value to gifted students, thus they need information about such programs as well as guidelines regarding how to choose these experiences for gifted adolescents.

Opportunities to Develop Habits of Mind and Attitudes

Often school programs for talented adolescents focus exclusively on helping students gain knowledge and skills even though research reveals that individuals who are successful in their careers typically cite other characteristics as equally, if not more, important than ability (Subotnik & Jarvin, 2005). Intrinsic motivation, persistence through setbacks and challenges, being able to take criticism, sheer hard work and practice, openness to instruction, self-promotion, risk-taking, goal setting and goal evaluation, social skills, the ability to work in a group, the ability to delay gratification and control impulses, resilience, and the ability to handle competition also are important ingredients for developing expertise and attaining desired levels of success. Typically, talent development programs assume students with exceptional abilities have these characteristics or will develop them in the process of going through school and/or special programs. These characteristics are rarely explicitly addressed or directly taught, but they

Table 1
Student Needs Matched With Program Type

	Special Schools	Dual Enrollment	Early College	Summer Programs	Distance Education	Contests and Competitions	Internships and Mentorships	Service Learning
Friendships With Intellectual Peers	✓	✓	✓	At least 2 weeks in duration				
Academic Challenge	✓	✓	✓	Specifically designed for gifted students	Specifically designed for gifted students			
Developing Independence	If residential		If residential	If residential				
Benchmarking of Skill/Knowledge by Professionals						If judged by professionals	✓	
Substantive Work in Field							✓	✓
Accelerated Curriculum	✓	✓	✓	✓	✓			

	Special Schools	Dual Enrollment	Early College	Summer Programs	Distance Education	Contests and Competitions	Internships and Mentorships	Service Learning
Taking Courses Beyond Scope of School Offerings in Talent Area		✓		✓	✓		✓	
Developing Specialized Talents	✓			✓		✓	✓	
Developing Organizational and Study Skills	✓	✓	✓	✓	✓	✓		
Cognitively Advanced but Immature				✓	✓	✓	✓	✓
Needing Tacit Knowledge About Careers						✓	✓	
Needing Motivation to Continue Study/ Practice						✓	✓	✓

may be essential in assisting talented teens. Through mentorship or internship programs, gifted adolescents may encounter adults who exhibit these characteristics or who can describe the role these traits had in their own success. Gifted adolescents also can gain awareness of the importance of certain habits of mind and characteristics through reading biographies and autobiographies of eminent adults. Subotnik and Jarvin (2005) noted how performing arts schools deliberately teach students how to handle critical reviews and lose gracefully, conduct themselves at an audition, and interact with potential employers. Many gifted adolescents will get instruction in these areas from parents, but some, particularly less advantaged students, may not, and schools and other special programs can address these areas.

Opportunities for Work to Be Reviewed by Professionals

Depending upon the talent area, critical review of the student's work by professionals in the field at key points may be very helpful in guiding the talent development process. For areas in the performing and visual arts, critical evaluation by experts before high school will help parents decide if school programs are sufficient for their child or whether special schools or programs through universities or other cultural institutions should be pursued. Evaluation toward the last few years of high school may be critical for the student to prepare and become competitive for highly selective colleges and universities such as art schools, dance studios, or music conservatories. Judgment of portfolios and musical repertoires by adult professionals can result in feedback not obtainable from even the best secondary-level teachers. Competitions also can be important venues where gifted adolescents can receive this kind of critique as well as valuable learning experiences.

Counselors Knowledgeable About the Characteristics
of Gifted Adolescents

Along the path of talent development, adults, especially parents and school personnel, who understand the unique characteristics of gifted individuals are needed to provide understanding and emotional support. Many school counselors assume that bright students will make it without their assistance, that parents of these bright students are especially interested in their development and will provide all of the necessary support needed, or that gifted adolescents have fewer difficulties or problems than their nongifted peers. Many may not be aware that some gifted teens, because of their extreme sensitivities, tendency toward perfectionism, difficulties finding true peers, clashes between home/community and school cultures, and the high expectations of their parents and teachers, may experience difficulties during adolescence and be at risk emotionally and psychologically. Counselors who understand the challenges that gifted teens potentially face can work proactively with parents to meet students' special needs in school.

Suggestions for Parents

Critical Messages From Parents

Parents play a critical role in the development of their talented teen. Research has shown that adolescents do listen to their parents and, in fact, obtain important attitudes, beliefs, values, and worldviews from them. Through open communication with their adolescents, parents can foster the development of healthy attitudes toward achievement, competition, work, stress, leisure, and learning (see Olszewski-Kubilius, 2008).

Viewing ability as something to be developed over time with consistent study and practice rather than as a fixed entity with which one is born (Dweck, 2006) is one of these important attitudes. Less than stellar performances and even failures need to be tolerated and sometimes embraced for their learning and growth potential.

Parents need to support their children's pursuit of a talent area even if it is not aligned with their own hopes and wishes for their child and even if it is risky and unlikely to be of high status or yield great monetary rewards. Parents need to be open to nontraditional careers as well as unexpected pathways such as not pursuing college immediately following high school or not attending at all. Parents need to push children toward finding their talents and own unique path of talent development while maintaining close emotional bonds with them and providing support (Csikszentmihalyi et al., 1997). During adolescence there is a simultaneous push by parents for their child to transition away from the family and toward his or her own unique, self-determined identity, while also maintaining emotional connections and closeness with the family. Parents need to communicate unconditional love, unrelated to and not dependent upon a child's achievements. Parents should allow adolescents to have their own views and opinions and encourage independent thought and analysis, even if it feels like a rejection of their own values (Olszewski-Kubilius, 2008).

Parents also can do much to encourage and facilitate the development of appropriate talent-enhancing attitudes in their adolescent, not only by what they say, but also by what they do. In addition, parents can model constructive use of leisure time, broad reading, cultural literacy, hard work, persistence in the face of setbacks, risk-taking, and management of stress. Teens who observe parents engaging in meaningful work, becoming involved in volunteer and service activities, pursuing political roles within the community, getting enjoyment and pleasure from participation in the arts, balancing work and play, trying new things they are not necessarily good at, and exhibiting good social skills and healthy lifestyles will learn many useful lessons that reinforce verbal messages from parents.

Summary

Adolescence is a challenging and critical developmental period. Important tasks that all adolescents need to accomplish include forming a unique identity, establishing independence from parents, finding a career or meaningful work, and establishing intimate relationships. For gifted adolescents, negotiating these developmental tasks often is complicated by factors unique to their giftedness such as parental expectations regarding entry into particular careers, prolonged dependence upon adults who provide essential resources for talent development, ambivalent feelings about being gifted, difficulties finding true peers, perceived tensions between achievement and peer acceptance, and personal characteristics such as emotional intensity, perfectionism, multipotentiality, and introversion. In addition, because of their abilities, gifted teens must learn to cope with the stresses of maintaining a high level of commitment to practice and study, which often involves sacrificing involvement in other typical adolescent activities as well as dealing with competition, extremely challenging work, setbacks, and even failures.

However, adolescence provides parents, teachers, and others the opportunity to assist, guide, facilitate, and influence the paths of talented youngsters. They can assist teens by providing the following: challenging learning opportunities inside and outside of school, appropriate benchmarking of abilities and achievements, guidance by adult professionals within the talent area, emotional support to bolster motivation and maintain commitment, and assistance in developing personal characteristics such as resilience and risk-taking needed for high levels of achievement. Armed with better knowledge about the unique characteristics of gifted teens and how these might affect their accomplishment of the major tasks of adolescence, parents and teachers are poised to make a meaningful difference in the lives of gifted adolescents.

Additional Reading Material

Daniels, S., & Piechowski, M. M. (2009). *Living with intensity.* Scottsdale, AZ: Great Potential Press.

Dweck, C. S. (2006). *Mindset: The new psychology of success.* New York: Ballantine Books.

Neihart, M. (2008). *Peak performance for smart kids: Strategies and tips for ensuring school success.* Waco, TX: Prufrock Press.

Distance Education Programs

Center for Talented Youth
http://cty.jhu.edu

Center for Talent Development
http://www.ctd.northwestern.edu

Education Program for Gifted Youth
http://epgy.stanford.edu

Duke University Talent Identification Program
http://www.tip.duke.edu

Kiernan, V. (2005). *Finding an online high school.* Alexandra, VA: Mattily.

Summer Program Guides

Online
National Association for Gifted Children's Summer Program Resource Directory
http://www.nagc.org/index2.aspx?id=1103

Peterson's Summer Camps and Programs Search
http://www.petersons.com/summerop/ssector.html

In Print
Berger, S. (2008). *The ultimate guide to summer opportunities for teens.* Waco, TX: Prufrock Press.
Peterson's. (2009). *Summer programs for kids & teenagers 2009.* Lawrenceville, NJ: Author. (Updated yearly)

Early College Entrance Programs

Brody, L., Muratori, M. C., & Stanley, J. C. (2004). Early entrance to college: Academic, social, and emotional considerations. In N. Colangelo, S. G. Assouline, & M. U. M. Gross (Eds.), *A nation deceived: How schools hold back America's brightest students* (Vol. 2, pp. 97–108). Iowa City: The University of Iowa, The Connie Belin & Jacqueline N. Blank International Center for Gifted Education and Talent Development.
Muratori, M. C. (2006). *Early entrance to college: A guide to success.* Waco, TX: Prufrock Press.
Olszewski-Kubilius, P., & Limburg-Weber, L. (2004). *Designs for excellence: A guide to educational program options for academically*

talented middle & secondary students. Evanston, IL: Center for Talent Development, Northwestern University.

Special Schools

National Consortium for Specialized Secondary Schools of Mathematics, Science & Technology
http://www.ncsssmst.org

Talent Search Programs

The Connie Belin and Jacqueline N. Blank International Center for Gifted Education and Talent Development, University of Iowa
http://www.education.uiowa.edu/belinblank

Carnegie Mellon Institute for Talented Elementary and Secondary Students, Carnegie Mellon University
http://www.cmu.edu/cmites

Center for Talent Development, Northwestern University
http://www.ctd.northwestern.edu

Center for Talented Youth, Johns Hopkins University
http://www.cty.jhu.edu

Center for Bright Kids
E-mail: centerforbrightkids@gmail.com; Phone: 303-871-2983

Talent Identification Program, Duke University
http://www.tip.duke.edu

Competitions

Karnes, F. A., & Riley, T. L. (2005). *Competitions for talented kids.* Waco, TX: Prufrock Press.

References

Achter, J. A., Lubinski, D., & Benbow, C. P. (1996). Multipotentiality among the intellectually gifted: "It was never there and already it's vanishing." *Journal of Counseling Psychology, 43,* 65–76.

Arnold, K. D. (1995). *Lives of promise.* San Francisco: Jossey-Bass.

Coleman, L. J., & Cross, T. L. (1988). Is being gifted a social handicap? *Journal for the Education of the Gifted, 11*(4), 41–56.

Cross, T. L. (2004). *On the social and emotional lives of gifted children: Issues and factors in their psychological development* (2nd ed.). Waco, TX: Prufrock Press.

Cross, T. L., & Coleman, L. J. (2005). School-based conception of giftedness. In R. J. Sternberg & J. E. Davidson (Eds.), *Conceptions of giftedness* (2nd ed., pp. 52–63). New York: Cambridge University Press.

Cross, T., Speirs Neumeister, K. L., & Cassady, J. C. (2007). Psychological types of academically gifted adolescents. *Gifted Child Quarterly, 51,* 285–294.

Csikszentmihalyi, M., Rathunde, K., & Whalen, S. (1997). *Talented teenagers: The roots of success & failure.* Cambridge, UK: Cambridge University Press.

Daniels, S., & Piechowski, M. M. (2009). *Living with intensity.* Scottsdale, AZ: Great Potential Press.

Dweck, C. S. (2006). *Mindset: The new psychology of success.* New York: Ballantine Books.

Dweck, C. S. (2007). Is math a gift? Beliefs that put females at risk. In S. J. Ceci & W. M. Williams (Eds.), *Why aren't more women in science?* (pp. 47–56). Washington, DC: American Psychological Association.

Eccles, J. S. (2007). Where are all the women? Gender differences in participation in physical science and engineering. In S. J. Ceci & W. M. Williams (Eds.), *Why aren't more women in science?* (pp. 199–210). Washington, DC: American Psychological Association.

Erikson, E. H. (1968). *Identity: Youth and crisis.* New York: W. W. Norton.

Ford, D. Y., Grantham, T. C., & Whiting, G. W. (2008). Another look at the achievement gap: Learning from the experiences of gifted Black students. *Urban Education, 43,* 216–238.

Ford, D. Y., & Harris, J. J. (1999). *Multicultural gifted education.* New York: Teachers College Press.

Greenspon, T. (2006). Getting beyond perfectionism. *Gifted Education Communicator, 37*(1), 30–33.

Hébert, T. P., & Kelly, K. R. (2006). Identity and career development in gifted students. In F. A. Dixon & S. M. Moon (Eds.), *The handbook of secondary gifted education* (pp. 35–64). Waco, TX: Prufrock Press.

Kerr, B. A. (1997). *Smart girls: A new psychology of girls, women, and giftedness* (Rev. ed.). Dayton: Ohio Psychology Press.

Kerr, B. A., & Cohn, S. J. (2001). *Smart boys.* Scottsdale, AZ: Great Potential Press.

Lee, S.-Y., & Olszewski-Kubilius, P. (2006). The emotional intelligence, moral judgment, and leadership of academically gifted adolescents. *Journal for the Education of the Gifted, 30,* 29–67

Lubinski, D., & Benbow, C. P. (2006). Study of Mathematically Precocious Youth after 35 years: Uncovering antecedents for the development of math-science expertise. *Perspectives on Psychological Science, 1,* 316–345.

Marsh, H. W., Trautwein, U., Lüdtke, O., Baumert, J., & Köller, O. (2007). The big-fish-little-pond effect: Persistent negative effects of selective high schools on self-concept after graduation. *American Educational Research Journal, 44,* 631–669.

Mickelson, R. A. (1990). The attitude-achievement paradox among Black adolescents. *Sociology of Education, 63,* 44–61.

Miller, L. S. (2004). *Promoting sustained growth in the representation of African Americans, Latinos, and Native Americans among top students in the United States at all levels of the education system.* Storrs: University of Connecticut, The National Research Center on the Gifted and Talented.

Neihart, M. (1999). The impact of giftedness on psychological well-being: What does the empirical literature say? *Roeper Review, 22,* 10–17.

Neihart, M. (2008). *Peak performance for smart kids: Strategies and tips for ensuring school success.* Waco, TX: Prufrock Press.

Ogbu, J. U. (1992). Understanding cultural diversity and learning. *Educational Researcher, 21*(8), 5–14.

Olszewski-Kubilius, P. (2008). The role of the family in talent development. In S. J. Pfeiffer (Ed.), *Handbook of giftedness in children: Psycho-educational theory, research, and best practices* (pp. 53–71). New York: Springer.

Olszewski-Kubilius, P., & Kulieke, M. J. (1989). Personality development of gifted adolescents. In J. VanTassel-Baska & P. Olszewski-Kubilius (Eds.), *Patterns of influence on talent development: The home, the self and the school* (pp. 125–145). New York: Teachers College Press.

Olszewski-Kubilius, P., & Lee, S.-Y. (2008). Specialized programs serving the gifted. In F. A. Karnes & K. R. Stephens (Eds.), *Achieving excellence: Educating the gifted and talented* (pp. 192–208). Columbus, OH: Pearson Education.

Pyryt, M. (2008). Self-concept. In J. Plucker & C. M. Callahan (Eds.), *Critical issues and practices in gifted education* (pp. 595–602). Waco, TX: Prufrock Press.

Reis, S. (1998). *Work left undone: Choices & compromises of talented females.* Mansfield Center, CT: Creative Learning Press.

Reis, S. (2006). Gender, giftedness and adolescence. In F. A Dixon & S. M. Moon (Eds.), *The handbook of secondary gifted education* (pp. 87–112). Waco, TX: Prufrock Press.

Rimm, S. (2002). Peer pressures and social acceptance of gifted students. In M. Neihart, S. M. Reis, N. M., Robinson, and S. M. Moon (Eds.), *The social and emotional development of gifted children. What do we know?* (pp. 13–18). Waco, TX: Prufrock Press.

Robinson, N. (2008). The social world of gifted children and youth. In S. J. Pfeiffer (Ed.), *Handbook of giftedness in children: Psycho-educational theory, research, and best practices* (pp. 53–71). New York: Springer.

Steele, C. M. (1997). A threat in the air: How stereotypes shape intellectual identity and performance. *American Psychologist, 52,* 613–629.

Subotnik, R. F., & Jarvin, L. (2005). Beyond expertise: Conceptions of giftedness as great performance. In R. J. Sternberg & J. E. Davidson (Eds.), *Conceptions of giftedness* (2nd ed., pp. 343–357). New York: Cambridge University Press.

Swiatek, M. (1998). Revision of the Social Coping Question: Replication and extension of previous findings. *Journal of Secondary Gifted Education, 10,* 252–259.

VanTassel-Baska, J. (Ed.). (2007). *Serving gifted learners beyond the traditional classroom.* Waco, TX: Prufrock Press.

About the Author

Paula Olszewski-Kubilius is currently the director of the Center for Talent Development at Northwestern University and a professor in the School of Education and Social Policy. She has worked at the center for 26 years during which she has designed and conducted supplementary, out-of-school educational programs for learners of all ages. She is active in national and state-level advocacy organizations for gifted children in the Midwest. She currently serves on the board of directors of the National Association for Gifted Children and the Illinois Association for Gifted Children and is on the Board of Trustees of the Illinois Mathematics and Science Academy. She has conducted research and published more than 80 articles or book chapters on issues of talent development, particularly the effects of accelerated educational programs and the needs of special populations of gifted children. She has served as the editor of *Gifted Child Quarterly* and as a coeditor of *The Journal of Secondary Gifted Education*. She also has served on the editorial advisory boards of the *Journal for the Education of the Gifted* and *Gifted Child International,* and was a consulting editor for *Roeper Review.* She currently is a member of the editorial boards of *Gifted Child Today* and *Gifted Child Quarterly*.

Printed in the United States
by Baker & Taylor Publisher Services